DATE DUE

8-5-82	SEP 0 7 2000	
5-29-83	NOV 3 0 2000	
10-8-83	MAR 2 3 2005	
5-15-85	JUL 3 1 2005	
7-12-86	APR 0 5 2006	
6-7-88	MY 0 4 '11	
7-27	FEB 2 1 2014	
1-8-89	APR 0 1 2014	
2-18-90	AUG 0 1	
FEB 3 1998		
APR 2 8 1993		
FEB 4 1994		
feb 28		
AUG 3 0 1994		
JUL 1 8 1995		
MAR 2 7 1996		
AUG 3 1 1999		
APR 1 2 2000		
GAYLORD		PRINTED IN

DIGGING UP DINOSAURS

For Hiroshi and Miyoko

This Is a *Let's-Read-and-Find-Out Science Book*

DIGGING UP DINOSAURS

by ALIKI

And putting them together again.

THOMAS Y. CROWELL · NEW YORK

OTHER *Let's-Read-and-Find-Out Science Books* BY ALIKI

Corn Is Maize · *Fossils Tell of Long Ago* · *Green Grass and White Milk* · *The Long-Lost Coelacanth and Other Living Fossils* · *My Five Senses* · *My Hands* · *My Visit to the Dinosaurs* · *Wild and Woolly Mammoths* ·

Let's-Read-and-Find-Out Science Books are edited by Dr. Roma Gans, Professor Emeritus of Childhood Education, Teachers College, Columbia University, and Dr. Franklyn M. Branley, Astronomer Emeritus and former Chairman of The American Museum–Hayden Planetarium. For a complete catalog of *Let's-Read-and-Find-Out Science Books,* write to Thomas Y. Crowell, Department 363, 10 East 53rd Street, New York, NY 10022.

Library of Congress Cataloging in Publication Data

Aliki. Digging up dinosaurs. (Let's-read-and-find-out science book) SUMMARY: Briefly introduces various types of dinosaurs whose skeletons and reconstructions are seen in museums and explains how scientists uncover, preserve, and study fossilized dinosaur bones. 1. Dinosaurs—Juvenile literature. 2. Paleontology—Collectors and collecting—Juvenile literature. [1. Dinosaurs. 2. Fossils] I. Title.   QE862.D5A34   567.9′1 80-2250   ISBN 0-690-04098-9   ISBN 0-690-04099-7 (lib. bdg.)

1 2 3 4 5 6 7 8 9 10
First Edition

DIGGING UP DINOSAURS

Have you ever seen dinosaur skeletons
   in a museum?
I have.
I visit them all the time.
I went again yesterday.

I saw APATOSAURUS.

1

I saw CORYTHOSAURUS.

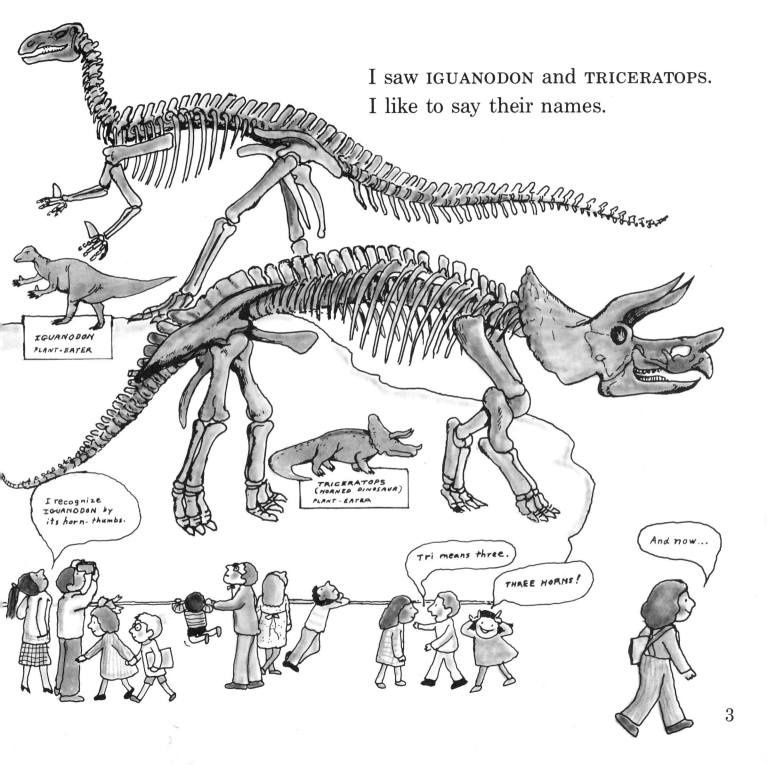

I saw IGUANODON and TRICERATOPS.
I like to say their names.

3

STEGOSAURUS was just where I had left it.
And TYRANNOSAURUS REX looked as fierce
  as ever.
TYRANNOSAURUS used to scare me.
I still can't believe how big it is.
Just its head is almost twice my size.

I'm not afraid of dinosaurs anymore.
Sometimes I call them "you bag of bones"
  under my breath.
I can spend hours looking at them.
I used to wonder where they came from
  and how they got into the museum.
But now I know.

STEGOSAURUS
(PLATED   DINOSAUR)
PLANT-EATER

The King.

TYRANNOSAURUS REX
MEAT-EATER

Dinosaurs lived millions of years ago.
A few of them were as small as birds,
but most were enormous.

ORNITHOMIMUS

TYRANNOSAURUS

Some dinosaurs ate plants.
Some dinosaurs ate the meat of other dinosaurs,
and some may even have eaten the eggs
    of other dinosaurs.

Dinosaurs lived everywhere.
The lived on every continent in the world.

Then they died out.
No one knows for sure why they became extinct.
But they did.
There hasn't been a dinosaur around for
    65 million years.

Until about 200 years ago, no one knew
   anything about dinosaurs.
Then people began finding things in rock.
They found large footprints.
They found huge, mysterious bones
   and strange teeth.
People were finding fossils.

Fossils are a kind of diary of the past.
They are the remains of plants and animals
    that died long ago.
Instead of rotting or crumbling away, the remains
    were preserved, and slowly turned to stone.

① 80 million years ago

Dinosaur dies and sinks into river.

② Its flesh rots.
Its skeleton is covered by sand.

③ In time, the sand and skeleton turn to stone.

④ Dinosaur is hidden for millions of years.

⑤ The earth changes.
Some of the stone breaks away.

⑥ 200 years ago

Part of dinosaur shows.

Fossils tell about life on earth long ago. Every thing we know about dinosaurs comes from studying fossils.

Fossil hunters found more and more big bones
in different parts of the world.
Scientists studied the fossils.
They said the bones and teeth and footprints
all belonged to a group of giant reptiles
that lived on earth for millions of years.
The giants were named DINOSAURIA,
or TERRIBLE LIZARD.

1822
Mary Ann Mantell found
the first dinosaur fossils
in England.
She discovered some
giant fossil teeth.

1825
Her husband, Gideon Mantell,
named the animal
IGUANODON, or IGUANA-
TOOTH.
Nine years later he
found an IGUANODON
skeleton.

1841
Richard Owen named
the giant reptiles
DINOSAURIA.

What finds these were!
People crowded into museums to see them.
But the dinosaur bones didn't just get up
  and walk there.
They had to be dug out of the ground,
  slowly and patiently.

Even today, digging up dinosaurs is not an easy job.
A team of experts must work together.

PALEONTOLOGIST

A scientist who studies ancient plants and animals.

GEOLOGIST

A scientist who knows the age of rocks and fossils.

DRAFTSMAN

Who draws pictures of the fossils.

WORKERS
Who dig the fossil
out of the rock.

PHOTOGRAPHER
Who takes pictures
of the find.

SPECIALISTS
Who prepare the fossil
for the museum.

15

This is how fossil hunters work.
First, they have to find a dinosaur.
They search along riverbanks and in quarries.
They climb up high cliffs, and down
    into steep canyons.

Dinosaurs have been found in quarries, where rock is cut for use in buildings and roads.

With luck, someone spots a fossil bone
poking through the rock.
The site is covered with a tent,
and the work begins.

Sometimes the fossil is buried so deep, the rock
  around it has to be drilled or blasted.
Tons of rubble are carted away.
Scientists chip at the rock close to the fossil.
They brush away the grit.
They have to be very careful.

As soon as a bone is uncovered,
it is brushed with shellac.
The shellac helps hold the bone together,
so it won't crumble.
Then the bone is numbered.

Sometimes a skeleton has to be cut apart
so that it can be moved.
The draftsman draws each bone in its
exact position, and the photographer
takes pictures.
That way, there can be no mix-up later,
when someone tries to put the skeleton
together.

21

When the bones are ready to be moved,
    they are carefully wrapped.
Small bones are wrapped in tissue paper,
    and put into boxes or sacks.

Large bones are left half-buried in rock.
They will be dug out later, in the museum.
These fossils are covered with a plaster cast,
    just as a broken leg is.

First, the parts of the fossil that show are covered with wet tissue paper, and then with strips of burlap dipped in wet plaster. Then the whole piece is wrapped in the same way.   When the plaster dries, it becomes very hard. The tissue paper covering makes the cast easier to remove later.

Each bone is then packed in straw, put in crates,
and taken to the museum.

At the museum, scientists unwrap the fossil.
They finish digging it out of the rock.
They study the bones.

Scientists dig out the fossil in many different ways. They use a hammer and chisel, fine needles, power tools like a dentist's drill, special sand-blasting machines, or even chemicals that dissolve the rock but do not harm the fossil.

They compare the bones to other dinosaur bones.
They compare them to the bones of other animals.
They try to figure out what size and shape
   the dinosaur was.
They try to find out how the dinosaur stood
   and walked, and what it ate.

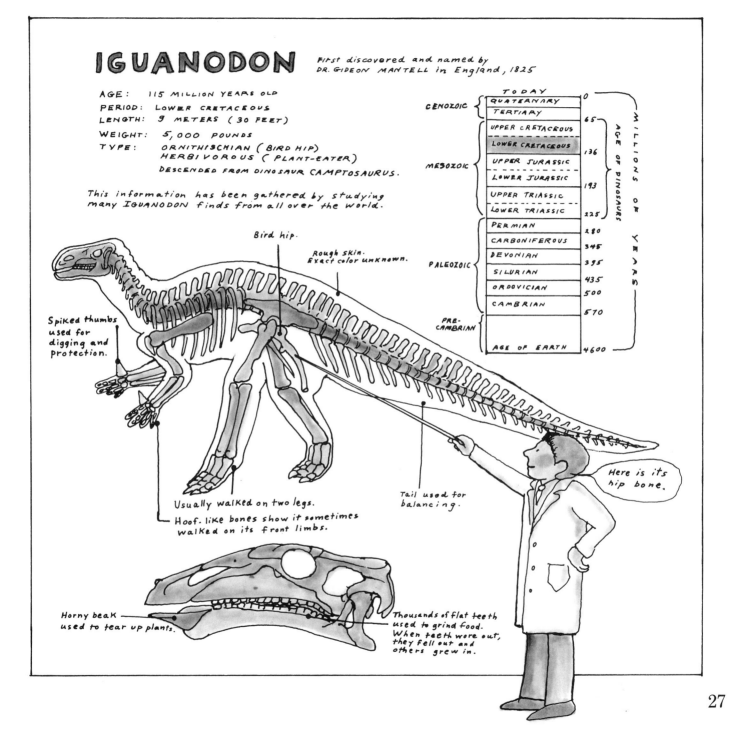

If there are enough bones, scientists are able
   to build a complete skeleton.
A frame is made in the shape of the dinosaur
   to support the bones.
The bones are wired together, one by one.
They are held in place with pieces of metal.
If any bones are missing, plastic or fiberglass ones
   are made to replace them.
You can hardly tell the new bones from the old.

After many months the work is complete.
The dinosaur skeleton looks just as it once did.

Until recently, only a few museums had dinosaurs.
Then scientists learned to make copies of the skeletons.
The copy is hard to make.
It takes a long time.
The original skeleton has to be taken completely
   apart, bone by bone.
A mold is made for each bone.

The new pieces are made of fiberglass.
A fiberglass dinosaur is just as scary as
   the original, but much stronger and lighter.

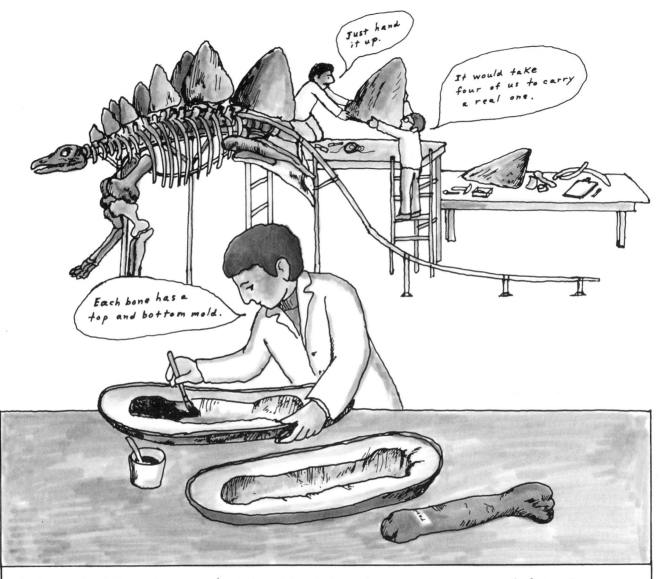

The original bone is covered with rubber latex and an outer coating of fiberglass to hold the rubber stiff. This is peeled off the bone to form the mold. The inside is brushed with resin and filled with fiberglass. Many dinosaurs can be made from the same molds.

Now museums all over the world have dinosaur skeletons.
And many people can spend hours looking
at them, the way I do.

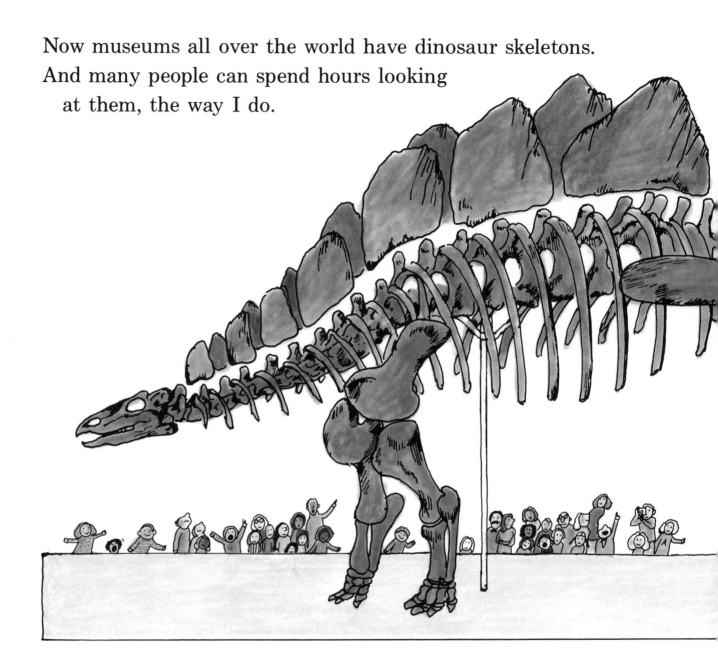

33

ABOUT THE AUTHOR-ILLUSTRATOR

Aliki has been fascinated by dinosaurs and their world ever since she was introduced to them by her two young children. Now that her children are grown, she wanted to write the book she wished she had had then to answer their questions—and hers. The author of many other popular books in the Let's-Read-and-Find-Out series, including *Wild and Woolly Mammoths, Fossils Tell of Long Ago,* and *My Visit to the Dinosaurs,* her *Corn Is Maize* was named First Prize Book for 1976 by the New York Academy of Sciences.

Long-time residents of New York City, Aliki and her husband, Franz, also a children's book author, now live with their children, Jason and Alexa, in London.